Horse Soldiers

Cavalry in the Civil War

by Jean F. Blashfield

A First Book

Franklin Watts
A Division of Grolier Publishing
New York - London - Hong Kong - Sydney
Danbury, Connecticut

Photos ©: Archive: 24, 29, 47, 48; Art Resource: 15, 39, 57; Cincinnati Public Library: 41; Corbis Bettman: 17, 22, 31, 34; Kansas Collection, University of Kansas Libraries: 8, 43 (top), 43 (bottom); Katherine Wetzel Photo: 37; Library of Congress: 54; Massachusetts Commandery, U.S. Military Institute: 19; New Jersey Historical Society: cover, 46; New York Public Library: 12; North Wind: 9; Photo Researchers, Inc.: 21; Photri: 26; R. W. Norton Art Gallery: 27, 38; 7th Regiment Fund: 55; S. K. Brown Military Collection, Brown University: 2, 53; Superstock: 11, 50, 51; Tennessee State Library and Archive: 6, 33.
Map by Accurate Art, Inc.: 28.

Visit Franklin Watts on the Internet at:
http://publishing.grolier.com

Library of Congress Cataloging-in-Publication Data

Blashfield, Jean F.
Horse soldiers: cavalry in the Civil War / by Jean F. Blashfield.
p.   cm.—(A First book)
Includes bibliographical references and index.
Summary: Examines the role played by cavalry, or horse soldiers, in both the Union
and Confederate armies during the Civil War.
ISBN 0-531-20300-X
1. United States—History—Civil War, 1861-1865—Cavalry operations—Juvenile lit-
erature. 2. United States. Army. Cavalry—History—Civil War, 1861-1865—
Juvenile literature. 3. Confederate States of America. Army. Cavalry—
History—Juvenile literature. [1. United States—History—Civil War, 1861-
1865. 2. United States. Cavalry—History.] I. Series.
E470.B64   1998
973.7'42—dc21   97-8525
                                                                          CIP
                                                                           AC

CONTENTS

Chapter One
Soldiers on Horseback

A rhythmic thud on hard-packed soil, a creaking of leather, a whinnying from a restless animal, then Charge! The clash of swords rings across the landscape as bugles blare and pennants wave.

Confederate cavalrymen attack a Union supply train.

This is the romantic vision of the cavalry, or mounted soldiers. Perhaps it stems from the so-called "Charge of the Light Brigade," which took place in 1854 during the Crimean War in Europe. This tragic event, in which hundreds of horsemen died, was immortalized by poet Alfred Lord Tennyson.

Mounted horsemen have always been viewed as the elite, or special people, of the military forces. The best of them had been training since childhood to be at one with their horses. Perhaps that is why the very name "cavalier" came to mean a very special, fearless, perhaps romantic mounted soldier.

In the United States, until the start of the American Civil War, the names "dragoons" and "cavalry" were used interchangeably. A dragoon rode a horse but fought on the ground, while a cavalryman fought from his horse. But in actual combat—or even in training—the distinction was meaningless.

Horses have long been used in several ways in war. They carried speeding men with messages. They carried leaders so that they could have a better view of the action and their marching men, or infantry, could see them. They also pulled wagons with supplies as well as

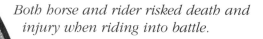

Both horse and rider risked death and injury when riding into battle.

gun carriages from which cannon were shot. Like people, horses died in battle.

HORSE SOLDIERS IN AMERICA

The United States military did not regard cavalry with favor. The existence of a troop of mounted men implied wealth and aristocracy, or elitism. This was opposed to the ideas of American egalitarianism, or equality—at least as far as the North was concerned. Southern aristocrats, because their slaves provided them with leisure, had the time and wealth to become cavaliers.

The first horse unit to fight for what became the United States was, however, a northern group. It was the Light Horse Troop of New York City militia, commanded by Captain John Leary in 1776.

Mounted men did not have a large role in the American Revolution. General George Washington frowned on cavalry, concerned that cavalrymen tended to think they were better than everyone else. He also thought that too much time had to be devoted to finding fodder, or food, for the horses. In places that had little plant growth, or forage, for the horses to eat, Washington wanted the forage left for the horses that pulled cannon and supplies.

The most famous cavalryman of that period was a Virginian, Henry Lee. He acquired the nickname of "Light-Horse Harry Lee" because the unit he led was called Lee's Light Horse. The

Light-Horse Harry Lee

term "light horse" meant that the unit used fast riding horses instead of heavy burden–carrying horses—and it sounded good.

It was Harry Lee's experience with horses that turned his son into an avid rider and fan of cavalry. That son, Robert E. Lee, grew up to be the military leader of the South in the Civil War.

AN EMERGING CAVALRY

In 1828, some traders traveling with a wagon train across the Southwest to Santa Fe, in the territory of New Mexico, were killed by Comanches. The trail was an important route for carrying goods to the long-isolated territory. Because the Federal government was trying to encourage westward expansion, the call went out for military protection for the Santa Fe Trail. Traditional unmounted soldiers—infantry—were sent west, but they were easily defeated by the mounted American Indians.

The United States Mounted Ranger Battalion was formed in 1832 to guard the Santa Fe Trail. Their year of service demonstrated the usefulness of such a unit. In March 1833, the first true cavalry unit in the army was established by the merging of the different companies of

As the United States Army's first mounted battalion moved into the West, the men faced Indians who rode their horses with great skill.

Mounted Rangers into the First Regiment of Dragoons. They were to work on the frontier, keeping the Indians from causing trouble.

The U.S. Dragoons, under Colonel Henry Dodge, were sent west in 1834. The men wore deerskins, but the officers wore the uniform made famous a century later in movies: a blue jacket over blue-gray trousers bearing

The nickname "Yellowlegs," given to the Dragoons because of the stripe on their uniform pants, followed the mounted soldiers when they became the U.S. Cavalry.

a yellow strip, up the outer side. This stripe gave the cavalry their long-lasting nickname of "Yellowlegs."

It wasn't the Indians that got the men of that first unit—it was the prairie heat and disease. In the first two months of the regiment's existence, ninety men died, but not one of them in action. The Pawnee and Comanche tribes chose not to fight the weakened soldiers, but they also refused to be controlled.

After several years on different assignments, the Dragoons gathered again in Arkansas in 1842. A new colonel was named, Stephen Watts Kearny, who was eventually put in charge of the entire West. For years, he and fewer than six hundred men kept much of the West safe for travelers.

In 1845, Kearny was ordered to demonstrate U.S. military might to the British who were attempting to take Oregon Territory. The Dragoons traveled 2,200 miles (3,540 kilometers)—to the South Pass of the Rockies and back to Fort Leavenworth—in ninety-nine days. They lived off the land and did not lose a single man.

Within months of their return, Kearny and his men were sent to fight Mexico, which was trying to keep the United States from taking over California, Texas, and New Mexico. During the three-year war, the cavalrymen acquitted themselves well. They captured New Mexico and California (while Texas joined the United States voluntarily). And they then helped to defeat Mexican General Antonio López de Santa Anna, whose troops had defeated Texans at the Alamo. After gold was discovered in California in 1849, the mounted soldiers returned to guarding the trails to the West.

STEPS TOWARD WAR

After Congress passed the Kansas–Nebraska Act in 1854, cavalrymen became involved in fighting their fellow Americans. Kansas was admitted to the Union as a state that would be left to choose whether it would allow slavery or not. Those for and against began to fight each other. They even set up separate state governments with separate capitals. Cavalry officers tried to use their troops to fight for the side they personally believed in, but the men who disagreed with them would refuse to fight. The cavalrymen came to serve as a buffer between the two opposing opinions, trying to keep killing to a minimum.

In 1855, Jefferson Davis, who was secretary of war for President Franklin Pierce, called up four new army regiments. Two of these regiments, the First and Second Cavalry, were formed in addition to the Dragoons.

Jefferson Davis was no longer secretary of war for the United States when the southern states seceded from the Union. Instead, he was elected president of the new Confederate States of America. Being a fan of cavalry, he counted on companies of mounted southern gentlemen to fight the war.

Jefferson Davis, builder of the cavalry for both North and South

The commander of the Union Army at the start of the Civil War was General Winfield Scott. He had been a hero in the Mexican War, but in 1861, he was seventy-five years old and rather set in his ways. Predicting that the war would depend on artillery, he refused to even discuss the use of cavalry by the Union.

Like the states, and even like some families, the officers in the existing U.S. cavalry regiments divided their allegiance. Well over half of the officers were Southerners, who quickly abandoned their U.S. positions when the Confederate Army was formed.

The cavalry of the Confederacy got off to a racing start in the war. It would take a while for the North to catch up. During the war, the Union raised 272 mounted regiments and the South raised about 137. In addition, there were many smaller, independent units on both sides. But North or South, the soldiers on horseback would play vital roles in the Civil War.

Chapter Two
The Cavalryman and His Horse

Not all army officers knew how to put cavalry to good use. During the first part of the war, when southern cavalry won virtually every engagement, the northern mounted men were not asked to do much more than ride as pickets, or guards, for infantry or carry messages. Even George McClellan, the general who introduced the saddle used by the cavalry, had plenty of horsemen but allotted only a few of them to each regiment of infantry.

Months went by, and infantrymen observed that cavalrymen saw little real action. They sneered that they never saw a dead cavalryman. Once the usefulness of the cavalry was accepted, however, commanders tended to send them out to deal with specific situations. A cavalry unit could quickly fill in a gap in a fighting line.

They could charge with swords and pistols or they could dismount and fight from the ground.

Cavalry activity often caught the public fancy, and songs were written about various raids. The cavalrymen had their own songs, too. In one of them, the men sang, "If you want to smell hell, jine [join] the cavalry."

An artist's drawing of a Confederate cavalryman riding picket. Riders needed shorter rifles than infantrymen did, but Southerners rarely had many weapons to choose from.

17

THE RIDER AND HIS WEAPONS

The U.S. Cavalry working in the West had found that sabers were close to useless against the Indians. They needed guns, not swords. They knew that muzzle-loading weapons were hard to handle on a galloping horse, so they asked for breechloaders—guns that could be quickly loaded through an opening at the back. As the Civil War began, neither side had many weapons useful to a cavalryman.

Cavalry guns had to be shorter and more easily loaded than the muskets and rifles carried by the infantry. Such weapons, called carbines, were scarce when the war started. It wasn't until 1864 that all Union cavalrymen had carbines. During the years of the war, the Union purchased more than 400,000 carbines of nineteen types. The Confederates never were able to give all their riders carbines. They had to collect the guns from Union dead on the field of battle or from prisoners.

SUPPLYING HORSES

A cavalryman without a horse is no cavalryman at all. Men could stay in the saddle longer than their horses could keep going on an expedition, so usually more than one horse per man was needed. One of the most difficult tasks for both sides was to assure a continuous supply of horses. Morgans were the favorite breed because of their endurance.

The cavalrymen of the South started the war with beautiful mounts, the result of long years of breeding. In

A pasture at a Union depot where horses were gathered and trained

the North, large horses built for pulling carriages were more plentiful than sleek riding horses. These mounts were not fast, nor could they maneuver easily.

During the first twenty-four months of war, Union regiments took delivery of almost 300,000 mounts. The men were often very hard on their animals, and those

300,000 horses were used by only about 50,000 men. Few of the horses were in good shape, yielding profit to no one but the men who sold them. Even circus horses were taken, though few of these animals trained to do tricks were useful in battle. Horses died as much from lack of care as from bullets. Infectious diseases were rampant. One unit lost most of its horses to hoof-and-mouth disease in only one week.

In July 1863, two years after the war began, the Union Army formed the Cavalry Bureau to supply mounts. Working from six depots around the East, they found horses, trained recruits in horsemanship, and took care of sick and wounded animals. One depot near Washington, D.C., had stables for five thousand animals. The Bureau paid the horse breeders an average of $160 per horse.

Confederate cavalrymen had to supply their own mounts, though they were paid a small fee for their use. If his mount was shot out from under him, a Southerner had to either steal another one or take leave to go home and find a new one. This became increasingly difficult in the later months of the war, when the battles moved into the home regions of the cavalrymen. At that time,

THEY ALMOST RODE CAMELS

In an experiment encouraged by Secretary of War Jefferson Davis, as well as an enthusiastic public, the U.S. Army imported camels from Africa and the Middle East in 1856. When the animals arrived in Texas, differences between camels and horses became apparent. Loading and unloading the beasts took practice, and the camels' loads often ended on the ground. Camels have good memories, and if an angry handler mistreated one, the camel would hiss and bite when it saw the man again. In addition, the odor of the strange beasts made horses bolt. One day, eighty-six camels got loose in Galveston, Texas, putting the whole town in an uproar.

Military leaders never quite knew what camels were good for—whether they should be ridden or used as pack animals or to carry artillery. As the Civil War loomed, they lost interest in the experiment. The animals were sold to the highest bidders for use in circuses and mines. Others were turned loose in the desert. The last descendant of the army's camels was seen in an Arizona desert in 1941.

*After battle, cavalrymen took along any stray
horses that they could muster, because their mounts were likely to be
shot out from under them.*

too, much of the forage for the horses had been destroyed, making it almost impossible to feed the mounts—though the horse was often allowed to eat before the rider found his own food. Confederate cavaliers often made raids just to capture northern horses.

When the war started, some Confederate cavalry officers took their body servants with them to war. But that bit of snobbery required that they supply and feed two horses for the one fighting man. Most servants were soon sent home, though a few officers made it through the entire war being waited on by their servants.

THE MOUNTED SOLDIER

The new cavalry recruit had a tough time. He had to learn how to ride, to manage his horse in formation, to care for the horse, to load and fire a weapon from the animal's back, and to use his lethal saber without damaging his horse, his neighbor, or himself. The rider had to be able to keep control of his horse in the midst of battle, when his mount, quite reasonably, was often terrified of the noise.

At first, cavalry recruits tended to load up their animals with everything they thought they might need. They soon learned that their horses could not handle a heavy load for any length of time. They cut their supplies down to a single blanket, perhaps a change of clothing, and an iron stake with a rope attached for tethering the horse at night. Once free of the heavy loads, a horse could travel 80 miles (129 kilometers) a day.

Horses died from gunshot wounds even more often than riders did because they made larger targets. A good horse—one that seemed to thrive on battle and work—

The farrier, or blacksmith, traveled with his forge so that he could shoe the cavalrymen's horses as needed.

was taken care of by veterinarians or farriers (horse-shoers) if it looked as if it would mend. Those who died were left where they fell during battle, but later their owners or others came along to burn or bury them. Records indicate that the farriers attached to the Union cavalry companies shod more than four million horses during the war.

Chapter Three
Cavalry South

Several Confederate states had cavalry companies before the war began, at least since 1857. The Southerners were used to horses, were good shots from the saddle, and also knew the terrain they would be fighting in because it was their home territory.

Union General William T. Sherman, in trying to make President Lincoln understand the southern cavalry, called them "young bloods . . . who never did work and never will. War suits them, and the rascals are brave, fine. . . . [They are] the most dangerous set of men this war has turned loose upon the world."

When Jefferson Davis became president of the Confederacy, his cavalry friends left the U.S. Army to fight for the southern cause. Such men as James Ewell Brown ("Jeb") Stuart and Robert E. Lee made the Confederate cavalry a devastating force.

At the first major battle, the First Battle of Bull Run (or First Manassas, as the South called it), on July 21, 1861,

The first major action of the Civil War took place at Manassas, Virginia. It was a victory for the Confederates.

the southern cavalry made a name for itself. Jeb Stuart's horsemen protected the infantry and scattered an important northern unit. The totally disorganized men of the Union cavalry spent more time chasing their horses that day than fighting.

A LEGEND IN HIS OWN TIME

Jeb Stuart had been part of the U.S. Cavalry in the West, serving six years in Kansas. Joining the Confederacy, he founded the First Virginia Cavalry. After the Battle of Bull Run, Stuart, though only twenty-eight years old, was made a general and put in charge of Lee's cavalry. Extravagant in all ways, he went into battle accompanied by a black banjo player who was instructed to sing of his exploits. With gray cape flying and plumed hat cocked, "The Cavalier" cut a dashing picture.

On a mission to Catlett's Station in Virginia in August 1862, Stuart failed to destroy the railway bridge that was his objective. Instead, he succeeded—despite a terrible thunderstorm—in stealing Union General John Pope's uniforms and money chest, plus papers that gave the

Jeb (for James Ewell Brown) Stuart, known as the "Cavalier of Dixie," seen at the head of his mounted troops

CIRCLING THE UNION

In June 1862, General McClellan's Union troops were near Richmond, Virginia, capital of the Confederacy. Lee sent Stuart, leading 2,500 mounted men, to gather intelligence information to be used in planning future actions. Instead of going back the way they came, Stuart, on a horse named My Maryland, and his men rode all the way around McClellan's forces.

At one point, to avoid being caught, they had to build a bridge over a swift river. After the southern riders escaped across it, they burned the bridge behind them. In four days, they rode 100 miles (160 kilometers), blowing up rail lines bringing supplies and capturing prisoners and horses in skirmishes with the Yankees. Stuart's men had ridden past 100,000 of the enemy and lost only one soldier.

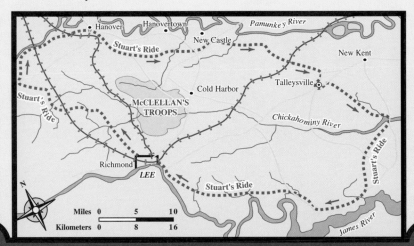

South vital information. They learned that a huge number of reinforcements were on the way but that if Lee's army attacked immediately, they would not be outnumbered. The Second Battle of Bull Run was the result.

THE BATTLE OF BRANDY STATION

Union cavalry troops, looking for signs that the Confederates were about to attack, crossed Virginia's Rappahannock River at dawn on June 9, 1863. They surprised a Confederate brigade and took many prisoners.

The Battle of Brandy Station—biggest cavalry battle of the war

But an even bigger surprise was that Jeb Stuart's ten-thousand-man cavalry was nearby at Brandy Station. Soon Stuart's men faced General Alfred Pleasonton's eleven thousand horsemen.

Sabers flashed and pistols popped as horsemen advanced and circled and advanced again. The action became the first all-cavalry battle and the largest cavalry battle of the Civil War.

The fight continued for hours, until Pleasonton saw the dust raised by the oncoming Confederate infantry. The general sounded a retreat. Stuart may have won that day, but Union cavalrymen had gained confidence. They would no longer be humiliated by the more experienced southern horsemen.

Soon after, Confederate troops moved north into Pennsylvania. The Southerners hoped to find new supplies. Instead, 160,000 soldiers battled for three days at the beginning of July 1863 in the Battle of Gettysburg, the turning point of the Civil War.

Without orders, Stuart took his men on their own mission instead of staying with Lee's army as it advanced. As a result, Stuart's cavalry missed the first day of the unplanned battle. He arrived on the second day, but Lee

The Confederate cavalry was expected to do what harm the men could, wherever they went. Here, they burn a bridge across the Rappahannock River in Virginia.

had already gone into action without the "eyes" he depended on for information. The South went on to lose at Gettysburg and never regained momentum. From then on, the war moved into the South's homeland, destroying it.

The following May, Stuart's greatly reduced and bone-weary cavalry took on Union General Philip H. Sheridan's much larger cavalry in the Shenandoah Valley. During the Battle of Yellow Tavern near Richmond, Virginia, on May 11, Stuart was shot by an enlisted man from Michigan. He died the following day. The

Confederates, disheartened by the loss of their leader, withdrew from the action, and by September, Sheridan had taken over the valley.

That loss did not long halt them, however. Brought back into action by General Wade Hampton, they stopped Sheridan's troops every time the Northerners tried to reach Richmond. During the next four months, almost twelve thousand cavalrymen—both North and South—were captured, wounded, or killed in Virginia.

THE LEGEND WHO LEFT AN EVIL HERITAGE

Before the war, Nathan Bedford Forrest had been a successful slave and cattle trader in Tennessee. Joining the Confederate army as a private, the burly Forrest quickly demonstrated that he could develop even the rawest group of riders into a daring, disciplined mounted fighting force. He was legendary for having almost thirty horses shot out from under him, though he was never wounded.

Forrest's superior officers admitted his skill but considered him insubordinate They sent him to Mississippi, where he was free to do pretty much as he wanted. In April 1864, Forrest regained Fort Pillow on the

HORSES AGAINST SHIPS

In October 1864, General Forrest took on the Union Navy during a twenty-three-day foray out of Mississippi. Following his favorite game of attacking supplies, he went after millions of dollars worth of Union goods stored at Johnsonville, Tennessee. With his horsemen on two commandeered steamboats, Forrest attacked the storage facilities. In a continuous rain of gunfire— and with the help of the wind—he set fire to numerous gunboats, steamboats, and barges, plus at least thirty pieces of artillery and 75,000 tons of supplies.

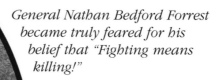

General Nathan Bedford Forrest became truly feared for his belief that "Fighting means killing!"

Mississippi River. Originally a Confederate fort, it had been in Union hands for the two years since the Battle of Shiloh. Offended by the fact that almost half of the Yankee garrison at the fort consisted of African-Americans, he ordered his Southerners to kill everyone they saw, especially black men.

The man known as the "Wizard of the Saddle" became one of the founders of the Ku Klux Klan after the war. For the next hundred years that organization clung to the southern belief that black people had no place in the United States except as slaves. Bands of the

KKK would harass and even kill black people, often hanging them from trees near their homes.

WITHOUT HORSES OR SUCCESS

After the defeat at Gettysburg, the Confederate army never again managed a major invasion of the North. Without new mounts, many cavaliers who had started the war so bravely found themselves walking when their horses died. Such cavaliers were often put into a behind-the-scenes company of men without horses, often referred to as Company Q. As the war went on, Company Q grew. An earnest rider hated being in Company Q and did everything he could to find a horse and return to action. But there were others who found it a safe haven.

The Confederate cavalry still had two years of riding to do before General Lee admitted defeat. The Union cavalry learned its lessons well, and during the final two years of the Civil War, the prizes of victory were theirs.

Chapter Four

Irregulars, Guerrillas, and Crooks

Cavalry units of thousands of men both North and South made raids into enemy territory, seeking information and damaging supply lines. But independent-minded officers and smaller units were sometimes formed to carry on their own guerrilla activity. Such men and their actions became very popular with the public, particularly in the South. Often the successes of these irregulars were all the southern people had to celebrate in the final years of the war.

One of the first irregular units was formed before the war began by Turner Ashby, a Virginian. Ashby's Mountain Rangers guarded the Potomac River crossings against raids such as the one led by abolitionist John

Turner Ashby and his famed white stallion

Brown on the arsenal at Harpers Ferry, Virginia (later West Virginia) in 1859. Ashby rode a white stallion, which made him seem ghostlike and added to the legend that built up around him. After the war started, many young adventurers joined him to pester Union troops. Ashby's company was so effective that it was soon incorporated into the army as the 7th Virginia Cavalry. Ashby was killed in battle in June 1862.

Two months before Ashby's death, the Confederacy officially authorized irregular units. Called partisan rangers, they were not quite official military but not quite civilian adventurers. Most such groups of men were neither efficient nor effective, and in the long run both the military and the civilians grew to dislike them. The main exception was Mosby's Rangers, organized by John Singleton Mosby, a Virginia lawyer.

John Singleton Mosby, the "Gray Ghost," and his raiders became the stuff of legend in the Confederacy.

MOSBY'S RANGERS

One of Jeb Stuart's scouts, Mosby sought independence from army structure. He gathered together a group of eight hundred enthusiastic men. They split into small bands of twenty or thirty to carry out whatever Union-annoying activity they could think of. They stole horses from encampments. They raided wagon trains of supplies. They even kidnapped a Union general right out of his headquarters.

After six months as irregular partisan rangers, Mosby's unit was incorporated into the regular army. New recruits were drawn to this 43rd Battalion by its apparent lack of regulation and its well-publicized successes, as well as the fact that Mosby let his men keep whatever "booty" they found on their raids. They stayed, however, only if they accepted the frail-looking leader's tight discipline.

At least one Yankee deserted to join Mosby. His northern voice allowed the Rangers to enter Yankee encampments before their true nature was discovered.

Mosby's Rangers were proud of themselves, whether or not they had a uniform to wear when they were photographed.

Mosby's tactics annoyed Union General Ulysses S. Grant so much that he ordered Mosby hanged if he were ever captured. The "Gray Ghost" never was caught, though several Union groups tried. He was wounded several times but always got away. In later years, Union General Sheridan acknowledged that his drive through the Shenandoah Valley was slowed considerably by Mosby's guerrilla attacks. For Southerners, Mosby's Rangers had "all the glamour of Robin Hood . . . all the courage and bravery of the ancient crusaders." Northern troops, however, saw them as cowards and murderers.

THE REBEL RAIDER

Just as foolhardy as Mosby was John Hunt Morgan. A Kentuckian who had fought with the cavalry in the Mexican War, he, too, liked to take his troops behind enemy lines to destroy and steal Union supplies. In July 1863, Morgan led 2,500 men across the Ohio River into Indiana and on into Ohio. They covered more than 700 miles (1,100 kilometers), skirmishing and doing damage as they went. Although he often destroyed telegraph lines, Morgan sometimes tapped into the lines first and sent fake messages that would confuse the Union troops.

THE HORSE MARINES

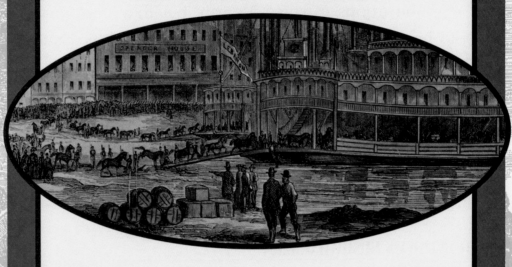

A peculiar unit among the Union cavalry was a troop organized by Alfred Ellett, brother of Charles Ellett, who had built a fleet of ramming river boats for the Union navy. The rams were vulnerable to guerrilla fire from the shores of the rivers. In 1863, Alfred Ellett formed a cavalry unit called the Horse Marines to ride up and down the Tennessee and Cumberland Rivers on steamboats. If they heard shooting, they stopped the shallow boats and swung landing ramps over to the muddy shore. The men rode their horses ashore to destroy everything, including houses, that might be useful to guerrilla snipers. The picture above shows an Ohio cavalry unit boarding a steamboat.

The North was in an uproar over the rebels invading their territory.

Union troops captured Morgan, but they could not hold him. The "Rebel Raider" escaped from Ohio State Penitentiary in late November of 1863, returned to Georgia, and recruited several thousand more men. They were on a raid in eastern Tennessee when northern soldiers surrounded Morgan in a house where he was sleeping. He woke up and tried to get away but was shot and killed.

QUANTRILL'S BUSHWHACKERS

Because of the Kansas–Nebraska Act of 1854, a generation of guerrilla fighters developed along the border of Kansas and Missouri. Those in Kansas who opposed slavery were called jayhawkers, after a fierce bird that did not even exist. Those in the South who fought the jayhawkers were called bushwhackers.

One bushwhacker disliked by North and South alike was William Clarke Quantrill. An Ohio schoolteacher who had moved west, he was already a killer when the war started. He had used the turmoil in Kansas and Missouri in the years before the war as an excuse to kill

William Clarke Quantrill (right), a northerner, was a raider-turned-marauder. He and his men burned Lawrence, Kansas (above), and killed many Union sympathizers while stealing all they could for themselves.

and rob in towns where the people were known to lean toward the abolition of slavery.

Quantrill and his followers fought alongside Confederate troops before being officially taken into the army in the autumn of 1861. On each raid, he killed captives rather than take them to prison. He tried to become an official partisan ranger, but the officers found his reputation was too unsavory.

In August 1863, Quantrill, then a colonel, led a raid on Lawrence, Kansas, which was the center of activity in favor of abolition. But this was no organized military raid. On Quantrill's orders to "Kill! Kill!", his men ransacked the town and slaughtered at least 150 men and boys.

This "fiend in human shape" was killed on a raid in Kentucky in May 1865, a month after the war had ended. He left behind a legacy that lived on long after his death. Some of the men who had served with Quantrill continued marauding after the war, freely robbing and killing as he had taught them. Among those who enjoyed the lawlessness were Cole and Jim Younger and Frank and Jesse James. They went on to become legendary gangsters of the Old West.

Chapter Five
Cavalry North

T he war was going to be over very quickly, so there was no need to recruit and train cavalry—so thought the leaders of the Union Army when the Civil War started. At first, the army was ordered not to accept mounted volunteers. Then, in June 1861, President Lincoln changed his mind because of the sheer numbers of volunteers who were being turned down.

Those inexperienced riders participated in the first skirmish of northern cavalry at the First Battle of Bull Run in July 1861. The seven companies of mounted horsemen were quickly driven into retreat by Jeb Stuart's men. That terrifying event quickly changed the minds of Washington's Union leaders.

By the end of August, at least thirty mounted regiments were part of the Union Army. Lincoln replaced the old, anti-cavalry general Winfield Scott with George B. McClellan. McClellan, an old hand at cavalry, was commander of the Union army for only a brief period,

General George B. McClellan, supporter of the Union cavalry

but by the end of the war, there were ninety regiments of Union cavalry. Even so, McClellan still did not use his cavalry to any great purpose.

GRANT CALLS ON GRIERSON

General Ulysses S. Grant, fighting in the West, was the first to put a Union cavalry unit to good use. He was trying to capture Vicksburg, Mississippi, the Union's last barrier to full control of the Mississippi River. Needing to divert the attention of the Confederates from his preparations, he chose a cavalry unit.

Benjamin H. Grierson was a former music teacher from Illinois who became an avid cavalry trooper. Setting off on April 17, 1863, from LaGrange, Tennessee, he led 1,700 men—each carrying only five days' supply of food—into Mississippi behind enemy lines to poke and prod at Confederate troops. They destroyed a railroad here, a bridge there, a telegraph line wherever possible, until they met up with Union forces at Baton Rouge, Louisiana. They had covered 800 miles (1,300 kilometers) in sixteen days, losing only twenty-six men. They distracted attention from Grant's movements, and they demonstrated to northern leaders that a cavalry unit could function behind enemy lines without having to be supplied.

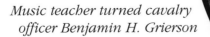

Music teacher turned cavalry officer Benjamin H. Grierson

RAID ON MULEBACK

At the same time as Grierson was leading his cavalry through Mississippi, a quite different "cavalry" unit was on the move. Ordered to destroy railroads in the high hills of northern Alabama, Indiana volunteer Abel D. Streight took bad advice and mounted his men on mules. The saying "stubborn as a mule" is based on truth—and most of the eight hundred mules didn't like their riders or their mission. Their mules became the enemy.

The ending of the raid was different from Grierson's, too. General Forrest of the Confederate cavalry followed Streight's mules, laughing the whole way. Finally, he tricked Streight's men into thinking they were outnumbered. They surrendered and became prisoners of war. Months later, Streight and some of his men were among the Union prisoners who escaped through a hand-dug tunnel from Libby Prison in Richmond, Virginia.

BECOMING A CAVALRY

Such raids as Grierson's encouraged the Union cavalry. A month later, during the Battle of Brandy Station, the disparate mounted units of the Union army became a genuine cavalry under General Alfred Pleasonton. They had learned what it felt like to be an integrated, efficient fighting unit.

Legend has it that the Union Army found papers indicating that Robert E. Lee was going to invade Maryland and Pennsylvania. The exhausted mounted men set off northward. One cavalry unit under General John Buford arrived in Gettysburg on June 30, 1863. They kept the Confederates occupied until more Union forces arrived the next day.

George Armstrong Custer has gone down in history as the cavalry general who made a "Last Stand" against American Indians, dying at the Battle of the Little Big Horn in 1876 in Montana. But the Civil War made him famous first. Because of his sheer recklessness, the West Point graduate had been made a general at only twenty-three years of age, just before Gettysburg.

On July 3, 1863, the third and final day of the Battle of Gettysburg, General Lee committed his infantry to

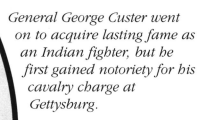

General George Custer went on to acquire lasting fame as an Indian fighter, but he first gained notoriety for his cavalry charge at Gettysburg.

one mammoth, 15,000-man charge that he hoped would break the center of Union lines. At the same time, the Confederate cavalry was supposed to ride around and strike the Union forces in the rear, but it had no impact on the outcome of the battle.

The 4,500 men in Custer's and General David Gregg's brigades took on Jeb Stuart's 6,300. In one attack by Stuart's massed riders, Custer charged at the head of his only experienced unit. The Confederates were forced to give way to the sheer ferocity of Custer's charge. His Michigan brigade became famous for continuing to fight after losing a higher percentage of its men than any other cavalry unit.

Cavalry, infantry, and artillery—both North and South—took part in the great three-day Battle of Gettysburg.

SHERIDAN AND THE SHENANDOAH

Even with the experience at Gettysburg, the Union's cavalry did not really function at its best until Grant put General Philip H. Sheridan in charge in 1864. "Little Phil" reorganized the cavalry, taking the men off picket duty and away from the task of protecting marching units.

Sheridan's men wore splendid short blue cape-jackets over a horizontal gold braid on a dark blue uniform. Their splendor earned them the derogatory nickname "Sheridan's butterflies," but their success in battle earned them admiration instead of scorn.

The Shenandoah Valley of Virginia was the site of

SHERIDAN'S RIDE

Still smelling of smoke after setting fire to much of the Shenandoah Valley, Union troopers made camp at Cedar Creek, Virginia, and General Philip Sheridan left for a conference in Washington, D.C. At dawn on October 19, 1864, Confederate General Jubal Early's men attacked the encampment, driving the surprised Northerners into a half-dressed, demoralized retreat.

On his way back from Washington, Sheridan was resting at the town of Winchester when he heard the distant thunder of gunfire. He quickly mounted his black Morgan, Rienzi, and galloped toward Cedar Creek. On his way, he met group after group of defeated men. One officer suggested they give up, but Sheridan exclaimed. "Retreat, hell!" And he convinced his men that they were capable of reversing the attack and going after the Confederates.

Sheridan's troops, taking heart from his encouragement, regrouped. At the sound of bugles, the Union cavalry became a juggernaut, driving the Southerners back. General Early later reported to his superior, General Lee, that his men had retreated in panic. "A terror of the enemy's cavalry had seized them. The rout was as thorough and disgraceful as ever happened to our army."

The North was enchanted with the tale of Sheridan's jour-
ney from Winchester. It inspired Thomas B. Read to write the
dramatic poem "Sheridan's Ride." Each verse brings Sheridan
five miles closer to Cedar Creek. Each verse takes another step
in changing defeat into victory. Read gave the great black horse
Rienzi much of the credit:

A steed as black as the steeds of night
Was seen to pass, as with eagle flight . . .
Hurrah! hurrah for Sheridan!
Hurrah! hurrah for horse and man!

General Philip Sheridan in his tent near the field of battle

almost continuous action throughout the war. The town of Winchester changed hands seventy-three times. The fertile valley was the source of much food for the Confederacy. It was also a route by which the Southerners could invade the North.

Given the task of clearing the Confederates out of the Shenandoah, Sheridan marched through the valley, taking town after town from the Confederates and killing Jeb Stuart in the process. That fall, hoping to keep the fertile valley's harvest out of the hands of Confederate General Jubal Early, Sheridan burned crops, barns, and many houses. The residents of the valley, who were left to starve, never forgave Sheridan for "The Burning."

General William Tecumseh Sherman and his mounted troops became the terror of the South when they burned Atlanta and then marched toward the sea, using or destroying everything in their path.

THE END

General James Harrison Wilson was given command of the cavalry divisions that General William T. Sherman left behind when heading for the sea after capturing Atlanta, Georgia. The 13,500 discouraged men were whipped into shape by Wilson, who led them into Alabama. Their destination was Selma, where the Confederacy had one of the few still untouched armories. On April 2, 1865, Wilson took Selma and then moved on to Montgomery, which had been the first capital of the Confederacy. As icing on the cake, Wilson's troops captured Confederate President Jefferson Davis.

Back in Virginia, Sheridan's cavalry was destroying most of the rail lines that supplied Lee's faltering troops. It was also cavalry units that General Grant sent, in charge after charge, to force Lee into a tighter and tighter space. He had to abandon Richmond, capital of the Confederacy. As Lee and his men headed toward Lynchburg, hoping to find one more source of supplies, Sheridan's cavalry and two infantry units cut him off. The leader of the Confederate Army had nowhere else to go. Lee surrendered to Grant at Appomattox Court House on April 9, 1865.

After the war, there was once again only one cavalry in the United States, the U.S. Cavalry. And once again, its main mission was to keep the West peaceful. The cavalry helped settlers take over America's frontier and turned the American Indians into captives in their own land.

The U.S. Cavalry rode through the Spanish-American War in 1898 and in World War I from 1917 to 1918. In

Lee surrendering to Grant at Appomattox Court House

that war, horses began to be replaced by tanks as the cavalry's favorite "mounts." The Civil War figures of Sherman and Sheridan became the names of tanks. In the Korean War and in Vietnam, the ready mobility of the cavalry, proved during the Civil War, was seen again as the U.S. Cavalry took to the skies in helicopters.

During the Persian Gulf war in 1991, a cavalry regiment riding in tanks and armored vehicles defeated an Iraqi Republican Guard Division in one of the largest tank battles since World War II. The First Cavalry Division, now assigned to tanks, still has a color guard wearing the familiar dark blue blouses and gold-striped trousers.

MAJOR EVENTS OF THE CIVIL WAR

1860
December 20   South Carolina is the first southern state to secede from the Union.

1861
February 4   Representatives from the seceding states meet in Montgomery, Alabama, and form the Confederate States of America.

February 18   Jefferson Davis, previously U.S. Secretary of War, is inaugurated as president of the Confederate States.

April 12   War begins at 4:30 A.M. by a Confederate attack on Union-held Fort Sumter in South Carolina.

April 15   President Abraham Lincoln calls for 75,000 volunteers to help stop the war with the Confederacy.

April 19   Lincoln orders a naval blockade of southern seaports.

July 21   The First Battle of Bull Run (or Manassas) in Virginia is the first important battle; it is won by Confederate troops.

August 10   The Battle of Wilson's Creek in Missouri, another Confederate victory, brings lands west of the Mississippi into the war.

1862
February 16   The fall of Fort Donelson in Tennessee to General Ulysses S. Grant's Union troops opens up Nashville to capture; Nashville becomes the first southern city to be taken by the North.

March 9   The first battle of ironclad ships, the *Monitor* and the *Merrimack* (called the *Virginia* by the Confederacy), ends in a draw but revolutionizes naval warfare.

April 25   New Orleans, Louisiana, is captured by a fleet under the command of David Farragut.

September 4   General Robert E. Lee's Confederate troops move into Maryland, invading the North for the first time and heading toward Pennsylvania.

September 17   Lee's advance is stopped by the Battle of Antietam (or Sharpsburg) in Maryland, in the war's bloodiest day of fighting.

1863
January 1   The Emancipation Proclamation is signed, granting freedom to all slaves within the seceded states.

March 3   The U.S. Congress approves the conscription, or draft, of all able-bodied males between the ages of 20 and 45.

May   The first all–African-American regiment in the Union army, the 54th Massachusetts, begins serving.

June 3	Lee begins another advance into the North.
June 9	The Battle of Brandy Station in Virginia turns into the largest cavalry action of the War; the North is forced to retreat.
July 1–3	The Battle of Gettysburg in Pennsylvania ends Lee's attempt to take the North. From this time on, the Confederates fight a defensive battle within their own states.
July 3	The siege of Vicksburg, Mississippi, ends in a Union victory.
July 8	Port Hudson, Louisiana, surrenders, effectively cutting the Confederacy in half as the Union takes control of the entire Mississippi River.
July 13–16	Riots in New York City protesting the draft kill or injure hundreds.
November 19	President Lincoln delivers the Gettysburg Address as a dedication of the national cemetery at Gettysburg, Pennsylvania.

1864

March 10	General Grant is put in charge of the entire U.S. Army.
August 5	The Battle of Mobile Bay in Alabama is won by the Union fleet under Admiral Farragut.
September 1	The Union army, under General William T. Sherman, captures Atlanta, Georgia.
October 19	After more than two months of fighting in the Shenandoah Valley of Virginia, General Philip Sheridan's cavalry regiments take the valley in the Battle of Cedar Creek, leaving the Confederates without an important source of food or a place to regroup.
November	General Sherman's army marches the 300 miles (483 km) from Atlanta to the Atlantic Ocean, living off the land and destroying everything the Confederates might find useful.

1865

March 13	Out of desperation, the Confederate Congress votes to recruit African-American soldiers. Five days later, the Confederate Congress no longer exists.
April 2	Richmond, Virginia, the capital of the Confederacy, falls to the Union.
April 9	Lee surrenders to Grant at Appomattox Court House in Virginia.
April 14	Abraham Lincoln is shot by southern sympathizer John Wilkes Booth. He dies the next day.
December 18	The Thirteenth Amendment to the Constitution, abolishing slavery, goes into effect.

FOR MORE INFORMATION

For Further Reading

Hakim, Joy. *War, Terrible War.* A History of US, Book Six. New York: Oxford University Press, 1994.

Durwood, Thomas A., et al. *The History of the Civil War.* 10 vols. New York: Silver Burdett, 1990.

Tracey, Patrick. *Military Leaders of the Civil War.* American Profiles series. New York: Facts on File, 1993.

VIDEOS

The Civil War. 9 vols. Produced by Ken Burns. PBS Home Video.
The Civil War. 2 vols. Pied Piper.

CD-ROMS

African-American History—Slavery to Civil Rights. Queue.
American Heritage Civil War CD. Simon & Schuster Interactive.
Civil War: Two Views CD. Clearvue.
Civil War—America's Epic Struggle. 2 CD set. Multi-Educator.

INTERNET SITES

Due to the changeable nature of the Internet, sites appear and disappear very quickly. The resources listed below offered useful information on the Civil War at the time of publication. Internet addresses must be entered with capital and lowercase letters exactly as they appear.

The Yahoo directory of the World Wide Web is an excellent place to find Internet sites on any topic. The directory is located at:
http://www.yahoo.com

The Internet has hundreds of sites with information about the Civil War. The United States Civil War Center at Louisiana State University maintains a Web site for the gathering and sharing of information: *http://www.cwc.lsu.edu*

The Civil War in Miniature by R. L. Curry is a collection of documented facts and interesting tidbits that brings many of the different facets of the Civil War together: *http://serve.aeneas.net/ais/civwamin/*

The National Park Service maintains sites on hundreds of Civil War battles. The directory of these sites is at: *http://www.cv.nps.gov/abpp/battles/camp.html*

INDEX

About the Author

Jean F. Blashfield is a writer with more than fifty books to her credit. Most of them are for young people, covering many subjects from chemistry to women inventors to England to World War II. She also has written several fantasy adventure stories and retold the stories of Gilbert and Sullivan operettas. She developed the American Civil War series for Franklin Watts with her husband, Wallace B. Black.

A graduate of the University of Michigan, Ms. Blashfield has been a book editor for many years. She developed three encyclopedias for young people, wrote educational materials about space for NASA, and created the Awesome Almanacs of various states for her own publishing company.